THE TWENTIETH CENTURY
LAMBETH

SUE MCKENZIE

LAMBETH ARCHIVES DEPARTMENT

SUTTON PUBLISHING

First published in the United Kingdom in 1999 by
Sutton Publishing Limited · Phoenix Mill
Thrupp · Stroud · Gloucestershire · GL5 2BU
in association with Lambeth Archives Department

British Library Cataloguing in Publication Data
A catalogue record for this book is available from
the British Library.

ISBN 0-7509-2038-6

Title page photograph: two ladies in The Cut, 1938.

 ALAN SUTTON™ and SUTTON™ are the trade
marks of Sutton Publishing Limited

Typeset in 11/14pt Photina.
Typesetting and origination by
Sutton Publishing Limited.
Printed in Great Britain by
The Bath Press Limited.

For Dad

Coronation Buildings, South Lambeth, 1960s.

Contents

The newly built Lambeth Town Hall on a summer's afternoon in a surprisingly traffic-free Brixton, *c*. 1910. When the Metropolitan Borough of Lambeth was formed in 1900 it was felt that the Vestry Hall in Kennington Lane was too small. The new town hall, built in the Edwardian Baroque manner with a 134-ft tower, was opened by the Prince and Princess of Wales in 1908. An extra storey was added in 1938, together with the Assembly Hall in Acre Lane.

Introduction

Old photographs are magical, they provide an instant window into history. There, looking back at you, are people from another time. People in fusty Victorian suits, cloche hats and funny swimming costumes, army and navy uniforms, drainpipe trousers and (worst of all) flares stare out with all the innocence of the past. Study the street scenes for people caught unawares, because they are the best: a man stepping off a tram; children staring out from an upstairs window; a cat asleep in the sun; captured and preserved, unknown to them, for us to marvel at.

This is a book of photographs of Lambeth and its people over the last hundred years. A London borough, south of the Thames, Lambeth is the sum of its parts. Each district has its own distinct identity and character. Kennington is a contrast of rich and poor with highly desirable squares and terraces juxtaposed against sprawling estates; Brixton is noisy, vibrant and brash; Norwood retains a Victorian air while Streatham is more twentieth-century suburban. Fierce loyalties exist even in today's transient society. Each area has its own amenity society, proudly protecting the rights of its residents and exploring its heritage. Districts within Lambeth have their own individual histories, dating from the days when they were villages surrounded by open countryside.

In order to understand the present we must look at the past. The shape and geography of Lambeth have determined its uneven development. The present borough, based largely on the ancient parish with the additions of Streatham and Clapham, stretches from the Thames to the Surrey hills and rises to 370 ft above sea level at Norwood. While the cities of London and Westminster expanded to the east, west and north, the south side of the Thames at Lambeth remained for centuries a desolate marshland crossed by a few roads raised against floods. A small village developed in the vicinity of Lambeth Palace, home to the Archbishops of Canterbury since the twelfth century. From the fourteenth century a royal palace stood at Kennington, built by the Black Prince and in use until the reign of Henry VII. The only bridge crossing was London Bridge, further down the river. Crossings to Lambeth were by boat.

The rest of the parish was open countryside with a few small settlements. The southern hills were covered by the Great North Wood, with its gypsy encampments attracting day trippers in search of fortune tellers. Highwaymen menaced travellers on the wild commons of Streatham and Clapham, which were established and fashionable villages by the eighteenth century. Samuel Pepys spent his last years in Clapham and Dr Johnson often stayed with the Thrales at Streatham Place.

Wharves and timber yards began to line the river front in the north. Potteries, boat builders, stone works and glasshouses relied on the Thames for power and transport. As industry increased the area close to the river became densely populated. The arrival of new bridges across the Thames in the mid-eighteenth century was crucial to subsequent development. Westminster Bridge was built in the 1750s, the first new bridge across the Thames for five hundred years: Blackfriars Bridge followed soon after. The Surrey side was now accessible and commutable. Wealthy merchants seized the opportunity to escape the sights and smells of the city and built large villas on the higher ground at Streatham, Norwood and Herne Hill. Houses began to line the main roads and villages expanded to meet the needs of the new residents.

The nineteenth century saw slow but steady development before the advent of the railways, from the 1840s onwards, which had a cataclysmic effect. The outlying villages were now opened up and cheap fares meant that city clerks could commute from Streatham, Brixton and Clapham. An unprecedented building boom followed and by the end of the nineteenth century, where this book begins, the foundations of modern Lambeth had been laid.

So how did Lambeth look at the beginning of the twentieth century? Walter Besant wrote *London South of the Thames* as part of a survey of London at the turn of the century. Written in the unavoidably patrician style of the Victorian philanthropist, it nevertheless provides a snapshot of Lambeth at the close of the nineteenth century. Besant describes the contrast between the north and south sides of the river with the magnificent façades from Somerset House to St Paul's facing 'low, dirty and half derelict wharves looking on to a welter of black mud'. Stamford Street is 'one of the ugliest and most sordid streets in London . . . full of dirty so-called hotels and disreputable apartment houses. . . . The New Cut is to the south, a noisy broad street, lined with gaudy cheap shops, with flaring, resplendent public houses, a loud-tongued market at the pavement's edge, and crowds of loafers, male and female, at every corner and lamp-post. Provisions of every kind predominate in the street stalls, fish and eel shops abound, while a large crowd constantly surrounds the cook shop windows.' The impression is of dirty, closely packed streets, some 'respectable', some definitely not, interspersed with factories, board schools and mission halls.

Further south in Brixton the picture is different: 'The greater portion consists of fairly wide but exceedingly uninteresting and drab streets, where middle class people of many types make their homes in the midst of the most non-descript architecture.' Drapers and bootmakers abound and the centre of Brixton is bustling and crowded. Brixton Hill is still well-to-do and there are market gardens in Lyham Road rapidly disappearing as new houses are built. Upper Tulse Hill has a lot of open ground, 'Elm Park with its haystacks and farm buildings'.

From Herne Hill onwards we see an area in transition. As London grew the wealthy classes, who had built their mansions and villas on the Surrey hills, suddenly found themselves surrounded by the hoi polloi. They moved on and the property developers moved in. Besant describes a scene in Herne Hill: 'The grounds of Herne Hill Lodge are all cut up into the smallest type of suburban street. All the houses are new, and the latest road, Fernbrake Avenue (sic), is still for the most part vacant as far as Poplar Walk, a few houses only appearing in the grounds that surround the property'. Streatham is generally blessed with a 'high class of house'. Norwood is a district of contrasts with bright clean streets, new terraced houses and tumbledown thatched cottages.

The building continued, only interrupted by the First World War. Attempts were made to alleviate the housing problems in north Lambeth by building estates in the south, much to the chagrin of the local residents. Denmark Hill was thought by one angry inhabitant to be 'quite unsuitable for people of the working classes'. However, most of the slum dwellers could not afford to move out to the suburbs so slum clearance and their replacement with modern housing became the order of the day.

The Labour-controlled LCC under Herbert Morrison came to power in 1934 with a manifesto for tackling London's social problems. The programme read like a prototype welfare state: housing, health and education issues were all priorities – especially housing. The LCC wiped away street upon street of slums, slapping on Compulsory Purchase Orders where they had to, and built modern council flats in their place. This was the heyday of municipal idealism and the 1930s obsession with outdoor pursuits and physical fitness. Lidos and paddling pools, bowling greens and tennis courts were installed in Lambeth's parks. Open-air entertainments were especially popular: Brockwell Park had its own open-air theatre. It was also a strangely nostalgic period. Perhaps there was so much change in people's environment in so short a time that they looked to the past for security. The song 'The Lambeth Walk', sung by Lupino Lane in the hit musical *Me and My Girl*, became internationally famous. People stuck their thumbs back *en masse* and shouted 'Oi!' Lambeth to them was cheerfulness in the face of the Depression, poverty with laughs, harking back to a world of cheerful costers and backstreet community spirit. It was such a craze, crossing class and national boundaries, that Mass Observation, the social and scientific research project, did a serious study of it and Mussolini reportedly demanded to be taught it.

Lambeth, like other inner London boroughs, was devastated by the Second World War. Over 4,000 homes were destroyed by bombing and another 38,000 damaged. Around 1,500 Lambeth civilians were killed and countless others seriously injured. Additionally many people were still living in houses condemned in the 1930s. The postwar period was dominated by a massive programme of public housing schemes. Slum clearance and rebuilding before the war had begun the process of change but now what the bulldozers didn't get, the bombs did. By 1951 the council had built the fourth highest number of new homes in London.

A need to break free from the horrors and austerity of the war years prompted a plethora of festivals, pageants and parades in the 1950s. The Festival of Britain was the largest but Lambeth had its own festivals as well. The Town Hall and Tate Library Gardens were floodlit, there were open-air dramatics and exhibitions and the Lambeth Regatta was revived. Free soil was given away for window boxes and Mayor Darsley launched a campaign to turn Lambeth into a 'garden borough' by planting flowers on bombed sites.

The postwar years brought lasting changes and the borough began its transformation into the multicultural Lambeth of today. Immigrants from the West Indies and Africa settled in Brixton. At a reception in 1948 at the Brixton Astoria to welcome forty Jamaicans an ex-RAF wireless operator told the meeting, 'We were completely disillusioned when we were demobbed in Jamaica after being assured that jobs were awaiting us. There was nothing at all. We all look to Britain for a brighter future.' The South London Press reported an unfriendly welcome at Waterloo station and not much better in Brixton where one couple told a sergeant at Brixton police station that they had relatives 'somewhere in London and please could you help us find them', and were told to make their own enquiries.

In 1965 the London Borough of Lambeth was formed. Streatham and Clapham, to the mortification of many of their residents, were transferred from Wandsworth.

In 1972 the Department of the Environment commissioned an area study of Lambeth, one of six commissioned to investigate life in the inner city with recommendations for change. One of the findings of the report was the change in the socioeconomic make-up of the borough. Gentrification of previously undesirable areas had caused an influx of middle-class professionals. Consequently house prices had risen, driving middle income families further south in search of affordable property.

Lambeth was notorious in the 1980s. Unprecedented riots against the police made the word 'Brixton' synonymous with violence and crime. Film crews and photographers were everywhere looking for more trouble while the people of Brixton tried to move on and build a future. The left-wing Labour council became the scourge of the media during the ratecapping protests. Lambeth was a byword for 'loony left antics'. The truth, as always, was slightly different. Inner city deprivation was rife in Lambeth; politics were extreme on both sides. The protracted struggles against extremism and corruption in Lambeth were, in retrospect, indicative of a transition from the old municipalism of the 1960s to the less benevolent but cost effective 'value for money' ethos of the New Labour council of the late 1990s.

Lambeth today is still a borough full of contrasts. Rich and poor live side by side. At Brixton tube station the chattering classes run the gauntlet of beggars and drunks every morning and in Kennington and Vauxhall sprawling, deprived estates coexist with leafy squares of desirable houses within the range of the Division Bell. And there is much in-between.

The time traveller would not have too much difficulty establishing his or her whereabouts. The main thoroughfares are still recognizable a century on. Many of the public buildings remain but with a different use: fire stations in Norwood and Kennington have become a theatre and an art gallery respectively, the synagogue in Brixton is a business centre, St Matthew's church is a theatre and restaurant, LCC board schools are now luxury apartments with fancy names and, to cap it all, to the chagrin of many Londoners, County Hall is a hotel.

This is not a comprehensive history. Using pictures, I have tried to create an impression, a sense of the times. Neither have the pictures been chosen objectively. This is my history too. My family came to Lambeth at the turn of the century and their history parallels the development in this book. In 1910 they lived in verminous cottages in Vauxhall, scraping out an existence and living in fear of the workhouse. This was a world far removed from today, a world of the cats-meat man and Italian ice cream carts, of pawn shops and Methodist mission halls. Children lived all their life in the street while glue and soap factories and Doulton's potteries belched out toxic fumes. They went to youth clubs and sports clubs set up by philanthropists and university settlements. They undoubtably danced the Lambeth Walk on numerous occasions. Slum clearance and hard work sent them to Brixton and respectability in the 1930s. They saw the horrors of the bombings and the borough's landscape changed beyond recognition during and after the Second World War. I grew up in Brixton in the 1960s and absorbed the cultural and social changes that immigration had brought to the area. I was on every demonstration in the 1980s when Lambeth was the place to be for a good march. Collecting the pictures for this book has been enormous fun, verging dangerously on the self-indulgent! There will be many omissions, hopefully not too many inaccuracies, for which I apologize in advance. The choice of photographs is entirely and unavoidably prejudiced by memories and experience: this is *my* Lambeth.

Most of the pictures have come from the Lambeth Archives visual collection, where I am archivist. The collection is impressive, a comprehensive visual record of the borough over the last 300 years, and Lambeth should be proud of it. Photographs give an instant impression of a time, a place, an event. They capture a moment of history. Some of the photographs in this book are official but the majority are personal. If you have photographs of Lambeth people and places why not take them to Lambeth Archives to be copied and added to the collection? In this way we can ensure that the collection continues to tell the history of the people of Lambeth. None of the pictures in this book is more than a hundred years old but look how different things are. Your photograph of your street, your school, a family event is already a piece of history – think how it will look in 2100. The borough's archive has also proved invaluable in researching for this book. Council minutes, local newspapers, the records of local societies and individuals all give background to the images. If you live in Lambeth or your family came from Lambeth and this book stirs some memories, then visit Lambeth Archives and find out more.

I would like to express my thanks to many people for their help and advice. Thank you to all my colleagues and friends at Lambeth Archives Department for their help and patience, especially Jon Newman and Tamar Baker. Thank you to all those who lent or donated photographs, especially Dave Stewart, John King at Railtrack, Mr Hancock at Surrey County Cricket Club, Ray Wilkie, Cath Mitchenall at St Luke's School and my mum. Thank you most of all to my husband Nigel and my children Sophie and George for their love and support.

Chapter 1
Into the Twentieth Century

Hungerford Bridge and the Lambeth river front, seen from Adelphi Terrace in 1895. At the turn of the century the river front was still dominated by industry – lead shot works, cement manufacturers, engineering works, breweries, sawmills and potteries lined the south bank. The tower on the left of the picture is the shot tower, built in 1826 and belonging to Walters, Parker and Co. Molten lead was dropped 163 ft from the top of the tower into a water tank to make lead shot for guns. The tower was in use until 1949 and survived until 1962. To the right of the tower is the Lion Brewery, topped by the Coade stone lion that now stands at the foot of Westminster Bridge. The Royal Festival Hall now stands on this site. On the other side of Hungerford Bridge the large square building is the India Stores, the military stores of the Secretary of State for India. As industry declined along the river front and factories were replaced by offices, many of the buildings fell derelict. The south bank was devastated by bombing in the Second World War and the whole area was redeveloped for the Festival of Britain in 1951.

When the Metropolitan Borough of Lambeth took over local government from the Vestry in 1900 they were faced with a borough of stark contrasts: north and south, poor and wealthy, industrial and semi-rural. People lived miserable lives in squalid slums in north Lambeth and Vauxhall while children picked blackberries in the country lanes of Streatham and Norwood and sheep grazed on Brixton Hill.

Joseph Priestley, Lambeth's outspoken Medical Officer of Health, reported a steady decrease in the death rate in the first years of the century, although predictably the rate was much higher in the north. Even so, there was a serious outbreak of typhoid in the Crimsworth Street area of Vauxhall in 1902, resulting in fourteen deaths. Priestley traced the source of the outbreak to an infected mangle belonging to a woman who took in washing. In the same report he also rages against the appalling conditions of dust heap workers. Several London authorities, including the Corporation of London, had refuse tips along the Lambeth river front. In scenes reminiscent of *Our Mutual Friend* people stood waist deep in unimaginable filth, sorting rubbish and extracting bones, metals and anything salvageable.

Turn-of-the-century celebrations were overshadowed by the Boer War. Troops travelling to and from South Africa passed through Waterloo station and local people would have been party to countless scenes of tearful farewell and joyful homecoming. The South London Press of January 1900 contains many notices of patriotic concerts and fund-raising events, interspersed with reports from the front. The dawn of a new century is scarcely mentioned. The usual pantomimes are there: *Dick Whittington* at the Kennington Theatre and *Alice in Wonderland* at the Brixton Theatre but the Canterbury offered a more patriotic evening with its spectacular *Briton against Boer*. The inmates of the Lambeth workhouse in Renfrew Road were treated to a variety show which included, in dubious taste, a rendition of Kipling's 'The Absent-minded Beggar'.

The housing situation was critical in the north of the borough. The worthy attempts of Victorian philanthropists, such as Octavia Hill, Guinness and Peabody, had failed to provide enough low cost housing to alleviate the problem. The Housing of the Working Classes Act of 1890 enabled local authorities to not only replace slums but also to augment their existing stock by building additional housing. The Duchy of Cornwall, a major landowner in Kennington, set an example in the years leading up to the war with a programme of slum clearance and rebuilding on its estate.

Further south the picture was different. The large mansions and villas of the Surrey hills had had their day. The wealthy middle classes had moved further south to escape the onward march of the great unwashed. In Brixton, for example, the large houses were now more likely to be converted into boarding houses or flats for music hall artistes and theatricals. Ninety-nine year leases expired on early nineteenth-century mansions with extensive grounds in Streatham and Norwood and speculative builders moved in, building street upon street of terraced houses. Road names such as Raleigh Gardens, Shrubbery Road, Hill House Road, Norfolk House Road, Baytree Road and Kingsmead Road commemorate the large houses that once stood on the site. In Clapham, on Thomas Cubitt's Clapham Park Estate, the grandest houses were suddenly surrounded by road upon road of terraced houses. Fields and farms that still stood on the southern borders of the borough began to disappear but the First World War brought the process to a temporary halt.

In 1914 Alderman Jabez Williams, Mayor of Lambeth, read the proclamation of the outbreak of war on the steps of the town hall accompanied by loud cheering and patriotic singing. The headquarters of the various South London battalions were packed with volunteers. The South London Press reported: 'At each depot crowds assembled to cheer the men as they arrived, while mothers, wives, sisters and sweethearts gave sympathetic encouragement to the khaki-clad defenders of their country.' Food prices soared, causing riots where women attacked shopkeepers. The two Lambeth workhouses reported that they had stocks of food for the next two months. Home defence armies were formed in Brixton and Streatham and the crypt of St Matthew's church was turned into a rifle range.

The war reports are almost eclipsed by a furious row over the LCC's plans to extend their tramways to run through the New Cut. This threat to 'London's cheapest market' caused an enormous outcry, with public meetings, demonstrations and a 6,000-signature petition. Lambeth Council objected to the scheme and it was shelved. There was also a lengthy debate concerning the increasing patronage of south London public houses by women since the outbreak of the war. The cause was put down to the fact that the government allowance for the wives of those at the front exceeded the normal housekeeping allowance and therefore encouraged women to debauchery.

Anti-German feeling was high from the outbreak of war. Wirtemberg Street in Clapham was deemed too German-sounding and had its name changed to Stonhouse Street. Many German shopkeepers were continuously harassed and the papers were full of 'capture of German alien' stories. Feeling intensified after the sinking of the Lusitania in 1915 and found its expression in rioting in the north of the borough. An enormous crowd, headed by boys singing patriotic songs, stormed through the New Cut wrecking shops with any German connections, however spurious. Shopkeepers placed birth certificates in their windows in an attempt to avoid the wrath of the crowds. One English man with a German-sounding name pleaded with the crowd not to destroy his premises in Lambeth Walk as his child was lying dead in a room above the shop.

Between May 1915 and September 1916 Lambeth suffered seven Zeppelin raids. The worst attack was on the night of 24 September 1916 when an airship headed north from Croydon. Streatham Common station was badly hit and six people were killed when a bomb hit a tramcar close to Streatham Hill station. Six high-explosive bombs and seventeen incendiaries fell over Brixton. Seven people were killed in Beechdale and Baytree Roads.

The war ended in November 1918 and Lambeth, like the rest of the country, celebrated enthusiastically. Dancing crowds filled the centre of Brixton and fireworks were let off in Acre Lane. Leave trains at Waterloo were besieged and police had to 'rescue' soldiers from the embraces of young women. When the celebrations died down and the soldiers and sailors returned home, the reality of a world changed forever and the pressing issues of unemployment and inadequate housing faced the people of Lambeth.

Queen Victoria's Diamond Jubilee procession passes along Westminster Bridge Road on 22 June 1897. Turn-of-the-century celebrations were a little subdued because of the Boer War but three years earlier London had celebrated with gusto. This photograph was taken from a window close to the junction with Felix Street and looks towards Westminster Bridge. The Queen's carriage can just be seen in the distance, followed by thirty-six English and foreign princes and the Life Guards. The South London Press reported that tall venetian masts lined the thoroughfare, draped in red, white and blue, with streamers and garlands high enough not to obscure anyone's view. People went to great lengths to get a good vantage point – look at the roofs and window ledges.

58 York Road at the junction with Vine Street, 16 July 1898. This photograph was taken from outside the Rising Sun public house. During the heyday of the music hall in the second half of the nineteenth century, many theatrical agents had their offices in this area until they gradually moved to the West End. Smaller agents remained, like the one advertised in the window, who catered for the bottom end of the market. Nearby was the York Hotel, where out-of-work actors would congregate and which became known as 'Poverty Corner'. The offices of the Music Hall Benevolent Fund were conveniently a few doors away. This part of the Waterloo district had a sleazy reputation for many years and was home to many lower-class lodging houses and brothels.

Dust sorters at Vauxhall, *c.* 1900. Those of us who equate dust heaps and dust sorting with Dickens and *Our Mutual Friend* will be shocked to discover that it still existed into the twentieth century. In 1902 there were three dust depots in Lambeth, belonging to neighbouring authorities. Workers stood waist deep in rubbish of all kinds and sorted it by hand. The depots employed mainly women and children because they could be paid lower wages than men.

Gunnell's Cottages, Salamanca Street, 1911. This courtyard was entered through a wooden swing-door, which revealed four two-storey cottages. At one time they were rented by a notorious dog stealer. On his death fifty dogs were found concealed in the yard. The drainpipes stacked up on the left-hand wall indicate that these cottages were next door to part of the Doulton potteries, who employed most of the people who lived in these streets. It is hard to imagine how this woman kept her washing clean as Doulton's were constantly prosecuted for smoke pollution.

Cows on Knights Hill, Norwood, September 1905. In contrast to the industrial north of Lambeth the south of the borough retained a semi-rural appearance.

Bakers Lane, Streatham, 1895. This was a turning off Barrow Road, near the junction with Streatham Common. The building on the left was the Orchard House Laundry, run by Ephraim Cox. The schoolboys looking on were probably from Streatham School, which was just around the corner.

Howell's grinding and crushing corn mills, Sufferance Wharf, seen from a barge on 29 July 1898. Sufferance Wharf stood at the river end of College Street, next to the India Stores depot. The site was cleared for the development of the South Bank after the Second World War and is now covered by Jubilee Gardens.

A horse drinks at a trough in Clapham Old Town, 1905. This was the main road through the old village of Clapham, as the name suggests. This thoroughfare retains a village atmosphere even today, despite changes to the buildings and heavy traffic.

The wedding reception of Marjorie Hoffmann and Arthur Murray in the grounds of Tower House, Leigham Court Road, in 1913. This house was later used as a teacher training college.

A day out from a Vauxhall pub, *c.* 1912. This could be a wedding party, a trip to the Derby or just a 'beano' to Margate or Southend. Judging by the state of some of them they are on the way home.

W.G. Grace at Streatham Cricket Club during Cricket Week, 1902, flanked by Messrs Barkworth and Beldam. The Cricket Club was to the north of Angles Road and was considered to have one of the most attractive grounds in England. The legendary C.B. Fry was a member. In 1921 the ground moved to Thornton Heath.

Flooding in Wood Street, later Dunbar Place, on Sunday 14 June 1914. The River Effra, by then a sewer, overflowed and flooded all the low-lying parts of Norwood. This was a regular occurrence until 1935, when the sewer was enlarged.

The Norwood Schools, Elder Road, *c.* 1910, a grim reminder of the Victorian welfare system. This was the infant workhouse, which was opened in 1810 as the Lambeth House of Industry for the Infant Poor. The building was added to throughout the nineteenth century and covered an extensive area. The workhouse took in children from all over the borough. Girls were maintained until the age of fifteen, when they were sent into domestic service; boys were apprenticed at fourteen or sent into the forces. When the Poor Law was abolished at the end of the 1920s the complex was taken over by the LCC as a children's and old people's home. Most of the buildings were demolished in the 1970s to make way for the Woodvale Estate but the 1840s schoolhouse remains and has been converted into private housing.

Brixton Road, 1910. Looking north from Effra Road, this photograph captures Brixton as a bustling town centre. As late as the 1870s Brixton Road was mainly residential, with the shops concentrated in Coldharbour Lane and Atlantic Road. As the suburb grew so did the needs of its residents and by the time this picture was taken, Brixton was buzzing.

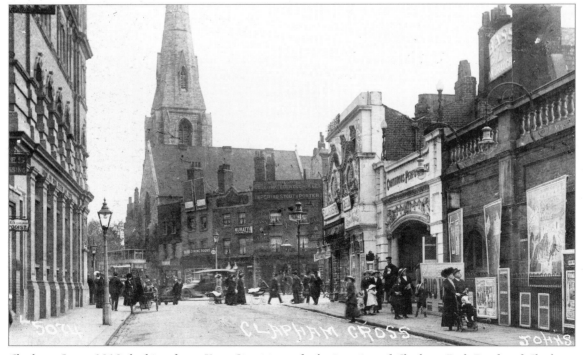

Clapham Cross, 1912, looking down Venn Street towards the junction of Clapham Park Road and Clapham High Street. The Electric Theatre is showing the Italian silent version of *Quo Vadis* and has dramatic scenes from the film displayed outside to tantalize the passers-by.

Cornwall Road, Brixton Hill, 1910. This road ran from Brixton Hill to Lyham Road and was renamed Blenheim Gardens in 1936. The sorting office in the foreground remains today but the west end of the road was demolished in the 1960s and is now covered by a housing estate.

A cottage in Elder Road, Norwood. This was one of three cottages, all dating from the late eighteenth century, that stood at the end of Elder Road on land that is now part of Norwood Park. When the park was laid out one of them was kept as a storehouse and survived until 1942, when it burnt down. In the nineteenth century the River Effra ran in front of the cottages and the road was reached by a little wooden bridge.

Pratt's, Streatham High Road, *c.* 1899. Pratt's was opened in 1867 by George Pratt, who had been a draper's apprentice in Bedford Row. In the 1920s the shop was sold to the John Lewis Partnership. The store remained in Streatham until 1990, when it closed amid massive protests from shoppers. Many people say that Streatham has never been the same since.

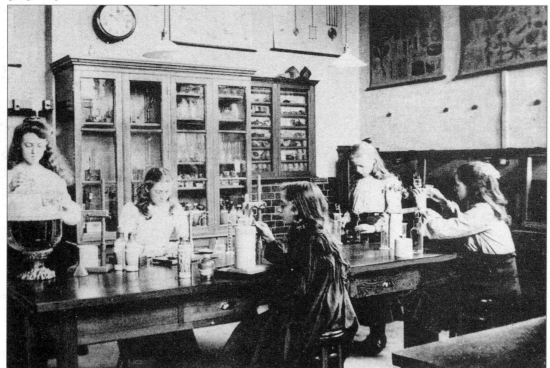

A girls' science class at Aristotle Road School, *c.* 1912. This was an LCC higher elementary school.

A view from Leigham Court Road, looking over open fields to central Streatham, *c.* 1914.

Leander Road, Brixton Hill, 1910, a typical example of a respectable lower-middle-class street. Leander Road and its surrounding streets were built in 1893 on the grounds of Raleigh House, which stood on Brixton Hill. In the 1880s the house and grounds were put on the market and there was a vociferous local campaign to turn the grounds into a public park. However, the MP for Norwood, Thomas Bristowe, campaigned more vigorously for the LCC to buy the grounds of Brockwell Hall and won. In fact Bristowe campaigned so vigorously that he dropped dead from heart failure at the opening ceremony. Little has changed in the road except that the houses on the right once backed on to the gardens of villas lining Tulse Hill and now back on to the Tulse Hill Estate.

A programme from the The Royal Canterbury Theatre of Varieties, 1909. The Canterbury, one of the grandest of the music halls, was developed in the 1840s by Charles Morton, the 'Father of the Halls'. It stood on a triangular piece of land bounded by Upper Marsh, Carlisle Lane and Royal Street. In its heyday it boasted a sliding roof, an art gallery and an aquarium. The reverse of the programme gives a real flavour of the times with advertisements for Dutch bookmakers, cafés serving stewed eels and mashed potatoes, tattooists and makers of artificial teeth. Acts that appeared at the Canterbury that year included stars such as George Formby (senior) and Harry Lauder, as well as an intriguing array of acts such as Hilda and Willie, the Bouncing Dillons, Frank Maura, the Mexican Wonder, Sam Elton – 'the man who made the Shah laugh', Biff Hall, the Melancholy Hebrew, Victor Wilde in 'Dodging the Missus' and Staig's steeplejack cyclists. When music hall declined in popularity, the Canterbury became a cinema. It was destroyed in an air raid in 1942 and was demolished.

The staff of Clapham Maternity Hospital, Jeffreys Road, in fancy dress in 1915. The hospital was opened in 1889 by Dr Annie McCall, a pioneering obstetrician. Dr McCall was a great believer in ante-natal care and natural childbirth. Single pregnant women were a priority at a time when the workhouse was the only other option. The hospital, staffed entirely by women, was renamed the Annie McCall Hospital in 1936 and eventually closed in 1970. The building remains and is currently home to a colony of artists.

A proper Italian ice-cream seller with boys from the Clapham Lads Club at their summer camp at Browndown, Hants, 1911.

Cinderella at the Brixton Theatre, Christmas 1905. The theatre was situated behind the Tate Library and had a narrow entrance that is now occupied by the extension to the Ritzy cinema. It was Brixton's first 'serious' theatre with weekly presentations by touring companies. In the 1930s the Brixton Repertory Company produced their own versions of West End plays as well as the ever-popular pantomimes. The theatre was destroyed by a high-explosive bomb in 1940.

Lord George Sanger's Circus in Norwood at the turn of the century. The eagerly awaited circus, with its big top and sideshows, came once a year to a piece of waste ground between St Louis, St Gothard and St Cloud Roads.

The Rayson family of Kellett Road, Brixton, in 1917.

The band of the First Surrey Rifles plays in Brixton, *c.* 1914, outside the Bonanza Stores on the corner of Brixton Road and Electric Avenue.

19 Baytree Road, Brixton, destroyed in the zeppelin raid of 23/24 September 1916. This was the home of the Lorimer family whose son, little Maxwell Lorimer, later became the lugubrious comedian Max Wall.

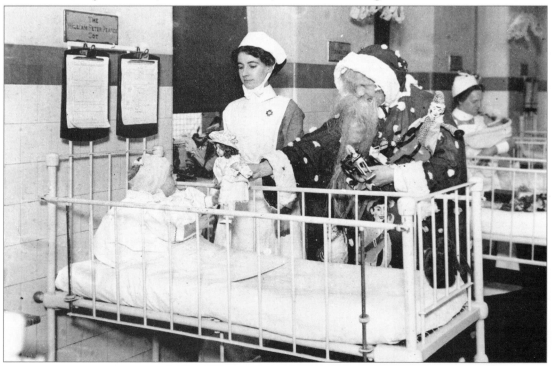

A dolly from Santa Claus on Christmas Day 1917 at the Royal Waterloo Hospital for Children and Women. The hospital dated from 1823 and stood on the corner of Waterloo Road and Stamford Street. It closed in the 1980s.

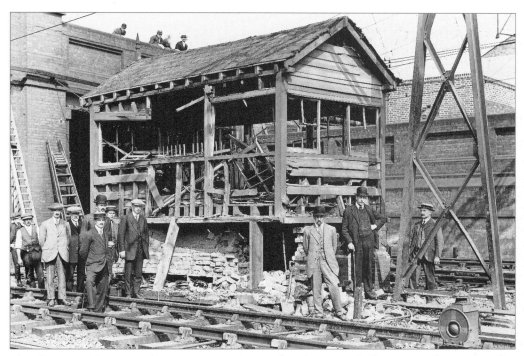

The shunting cabin, Streatham Common station, after the air raid of 24 September 1916. The Zeppelin dropped thirty-two bombs on Streatham, killing seven people and seriously injuring twenty-seven. When a bomb fell in Estreham Road the railway station took the full impact.

Mr and Mrs Walter Drayson and Prince, hero of a Zeppelin raid on Natal Road, Streatham. Prince could apparently predict impending air raids and had been particularly restless on the evening of 24 September. He was proved right when an incendiary bomb fell close to his kennel, sending up flames 6 ft high. Prince alerted Mr Drayson and the flames were extinguished. The neighbours were so grateful that they presented Prince with an engraved collar. The story has a grisly postscript, however: when Prince died he was stuffed and presented in a glass case, along with the bomb and the collar, to the Streatham Antiquarian Society.

The crypt of St Luke's church, West Norwood, in 1916. The crypt was used as an air raid shelter during the First World War. The man standing in the centre of the picture is Alfred Vincent, Norwood ironmonger and head of the local St John's Ambulance Brigade.

This sullen-looking bunch are the Mckenzie boys of Frank Street, Kennington, in 1914. The boy in the hat on the left is Alec who, like many boys, lied about his age so he could enlist in the army at fifteen. The young man in the naval uniform is their Uncle Albert who became a local hero when he was awarded the VC for his bravery at the Battle of Zeebrugge. He died in 1918 during the influenza epidemic, aged only twenty.

Waterloo station in July 1919, during victory celebrations. Soldiers departed and returned via Waterloo during the Boer War. When war broke out it delayed the rebuilding of the station, which had begun in 1904 after extensive slum clearance in the area. The new station, complete with Victory Arch, was opened by Queen Mary in 1922.

Peace celebrations in Kennington Park, 19 July 1919. Celebrations and pageants were held in most of Lambeth's parks.

Messrs Green (right) and Nelson, war veterans, recuperating at the Cedars Road Hospital, Clapham, 1918.

Chapter 2
The Skies Ain't Blue,
The Grass Ain't Green

A street in the Waterloo area, *c.* 1925. Many grim streets in this area were demolished to make way for County Hall and others were swept away in local authority slum clearance schemes. Basement rooms were deemed to be unfit for human habitation at the turn of the century, mainly because of leaking sewage during heavy rainfalls; however, a survey of 1930 showed that at least 100,000 Londoners were still living in them.

The years between the wars saw many changes in Lambeth's landscape. New housing estates replaced many of the slums in the north and suburban houses covered the remaining open land of Streatham and Norwood.

In 1919 Joseph Priestley, Lambeth's Medical Officer of Health, submitted a social housing report to the Ministry of Health. In the report he opposed the building of tenement blocks in the north of the borough as had been done in the past. Priestley believed that new housing schemes should be of the 'cottage' variety, built on the outskirts of the borough, away from polluted industrial centres. Three sites in Norwood were identified, the grounds of Portobello House, Holderness House and a site in St Gothard's road. He also suggested that large houses in the borough should be converted into flats. The flaw in this was that many people, especially people of 'the lowest classes', were reluctant to move out of their street, never mind to a whole new district. Although the cottage estates served a purpose they did little to relieve the housing crisis in the north. By the end of the 1920s the emphasis had moved to slum clearance and replacement public housing on the same sites. The LCC's 'post-office Georgian' China Walk Estate of 1929 was the first. The original design included gardens, tennis courts and lily ponds but the impact of the Depression on the LCC's finances left bleak tarmac courtyards. China Walk was followed by housing estates in south Lambeth and Kennington in the 1930s. Large estates were also planned in outlying areas such as Tulse Hill and in Poynders Road, Clapham, where there was such an outcry from local residents that the idea was temporarily shelved.

In January 1928 the Thames burst its banks, flooding the riverside streets. College Street and Stamford Street were particularly badly affected. No one was drowned, unlike on the Westminster side where people were drowned in their basement bedrooms, but homes and belongings were destroyed. The South London Press reported, 'Resigned stoicism was shown by the hundreds of poor Lambeth people of the struggling working classes who had lost in a few minutes what had taken a lifetime to build up'.

Llewellyn's *New Survey of London Labour* of 1930 noted that, in Lambeth, 'The density of the houses and the social grade of the inhabitants are related to the elevation of the land'. The study produced a map of social status, a comparison with Booth's map of the 1890s. It showed many improvements; there were not so many rough streets on the map although those that remained were concentrated in the north. The survey cited the poorest and most dangerous streets in the borough as Old Paradise Street off Lambeth Walk, Waxwell Terrace off Westminster Bridge Road, Nelson's Row and White's Square in Clapham and Cranworth Gardens in Brixton. Slums persisted, basement rooms that had long been declared unfit for human habitation because of leaking sewage during flooding were still in use. The Ministry of Health estimated that over 100,000 Londoners were still living in basement rooms.

There was a great emphasis on physical fitness and outdoor pursuits in the 1930s. Open-air swimming pools were built in Brockwell and Kennington Parks, allowing unrestricted mixed bathing for the first time, and indoor pools opened at Clapham and Streatham. Municipal tennis courts and bowling greens abounded. The church youth clubs and the university settlements in the poorer areas laid great emphasis on sports, with boxing matches, football and cricket teams, cycling and rambling clubs. Spectator sports were also hugely popular, and attendance at cricket and football matches was at its highest. Crowds packed the Oval in the summer. (Until the boom in attendance in 1934 the ground had been surrounded by a wooden fence; men with sticks were employed to patrol the perimeter and deter small boys who, anxious for a glimpse of Jack Hobbs, tried to climb over.) Brixton boasted a short-lived greyhound racing track in the mid-1930s, speedway racing was immensely popular at Crystal Palace and a cycling track was built at Herne Hill. Skating was popular too: one could roller skate at the rink on the corner of Tulse Hill and Water Lane or ice skate at the new rink at Streatham.

Even the cult of naturism reached parts of Lambeth. In 1930 South London Press reporters visited a house in Stockwell Green occupied by a family of nudists – the Potters. A picture of the family – above the waist – with Mr Potter smoking a pipe and Mrs Potter discreetly airbrushed, appeared on the front page and caused much consternation among the readers. One outraged correspondent was offered a 'hot' picture by a schoolboy and was horrified to discover that it was a cutting from the local newspaper.

Music hall had been replaced by cinema as the great panacea. In 1929 there were twenty-one cinemas in Lambeth alone, not counting Streatham and Clapham. Films were interspersed with live acts: at the Trocadero at the Elephant and Castle you could watch a Ronald Colman film *and* see Louis Armstrong and his band live on stage. The Brixton Astoria opened in 1929, with an interior reminiscent of an Italian garden, complete with a balcony and moonlit sky. Development along the west side of Streatham Hill, which resulted in the Locarno dance hall, the Gaumont Palace cinema and the Streatham Hill Theatre, endowed Streatham with the title 'entertainment centre of South London'. Shopping was on a large scale too. This was the era of the department store: Bon Marché, Morley's and Quin & Axten's in Brixton, Pratt's in Streatham, and Arding and Hobbs at Clapham Junction.

The interwar years are unique in that they have a clear beginning and an end. They have an innate poignancy; we know in retrospect that years of misery and then austerity were to follow. Lambeth's landscape was already changing – slum clearance and extensive building programmes had ensured that. The next six years speeded up that change.

Lambeth Bridge and the river front, 1928. Built in 1862 to replace the ferry, the iron bridge had become a rusty eyesore and was closed to traffic in 1910. The old bridge was demolished in 1929, after a temporary structure was erected, and the new bridge was completed in 1932.

The Old Vic, *c.* 1920. This theatre was built in 1816 on a swampy site using stone from the Savoy Palace, which had recently been demolished to make way for Waterloo Bridge. The theatre had an auspicious start but it rapidly declined after the 1830s – it began showing crude melodramas and acquired a shady reputation. In 1879 Emma Cons persuaded the Coffee Palace Association to buy the financially precarious theatre and it became the Royal Victoria Coffee Music Hall. After Emma Cons' death in 1912 her niece Lilian Baylis ran the theatre, putting on Shakespeare at prices ordinary people could afford. Children were encouraged to watch with sweets and oranges, which were only given to them on leaving the theatre. However, attempts to educate the masses were sometimes in vain. Boys from a Vauxhall school attended a performance of the *Merchant of Venice* in 1918, at the height of meat rationing. When Shylock demanded his pound of flesh a voice from the audience shouted to the Duke of Milan, 'Oi you, ask him for his meat ticket' and brought the house down.

Vauxhall Cross in 1920. Here is proof that some things never change. This junction of five major roads –
Vauxhall Bridge, Harleyford Road, South Lambeth Road, Wandsworth Road and Albert Embankment – has
always been a traffic nightmare!

Walnut Tree Walk school football team, 1920.

A novelty postcard from the Crystal Palace that shows what went on there after dark!

The Crystal Palace in the 1920s. By the turn of the century the palace, always a financial liability, was in decline. Despite the success of the Festival of Empire in 1911 the company went bankrupt and the palace was bought for the nation. It was used as a naval barracks during the First World War and reopened to the public in 1920. The Crystal Palace never regained its former glory but was a popular venue in the interwar years for concerts, speedway racing, dog and cat shows and outside firework displays.

Bathing in a lake in Brockwell Park in the 1920s. The lake was immensely popular but swimmers had to contend with model boats and stagnant water. It was eventually deemed too unhygienic and was superceded by the Lido.

A May Day festival in Railton Road, 1935.

Lambeth Mission in the 1930s. The 'Ideal' cinema was the brainchild of the Revd Thomas Tiplady and was the mission's successful attempt to boost rapidly dwindling congregations. Tiplady recognized the popular appeal of the cinema and it was a turning point in the fortunes of the Mission, as you can see from the huge crowds. The cinema was destroyed in the Second World War.

Lambeth Mission Life Boys, *c.* 1930.

St Luke's School centenary celebrations, 1925. The West Norwood school is one of the oldest in Lambeth and in 1925 celebrated its centenary by photographing the oldest surviving ex-pupils with the school's youngest. These old men would have been at the school in the 1860s.

Empire Day at St Luke's in the 1920s.

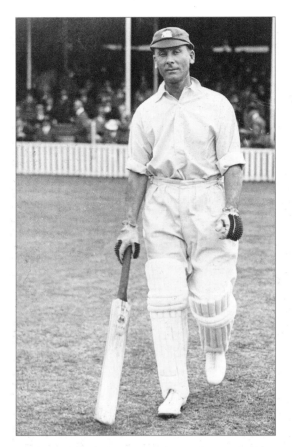

Every schoolboy's hero – Jack Hobbs coming out to bat. Cambridge-born Jack Hobbs joined Surrey County Cricket Club in 1903. Even though he had no formal cricket coaching he became one of the most successful and best-loved cricketers of all time. He retired in 1934 with a career average of 50.65, having scored 197 centuries, 98 of those when he was over 40. He was the first professional cricketer to be knighted in 1953. An unassuming and deeply religious man, he was loved for his ordinariness and lack of pretension and took obvious pleasure in his achievement. The Hobbs Gates at the Oval were erected in his memory.

A Kennington boys' club boxing team, c. 1928.

A salt seller, Lower Marsh, 1938. The New Cut, renamed The Cut in the 1930s, and Lower Marsh street market were two of the largest and roughest of the Victorian markets. Mary Benedetta, writing in *The Street Markets of London* in 1936 must have visited Lower Marsh on a particularly bad day. She was appalled by what she saw, describing it as 'unsavoury' with a 'forbidding atmosphere as if it threatens you not to find out too much. Opposite the stalls the houses are blackened and decayed, their windows silted up with grime and their doors closed unwelcomingly, with filth thick in every crevice.'

Scenes from The Cut, 1938.

Woolworth's on Brixton Road in the 1920s. The store originally stood on the corner of Brixton Road and Atlantic Road. A new art deco-style store was built further along Brixton Road when it was widened in 1936.

David Greig, the grocers, was a familiar site and there were shops all over south London. The first shop opened in Atlantic Road, Brixton, in the 1880s.

Charles Kingston at the door of his removal and second-hand business in Electric Lane, Brixton, *c.* 1930.

Morley's of Brixton in the 1920s. The impressive arcade was eventually dismantled to make room for an increased sales area. Morley's remains in Brixton today as its only surviving department store.

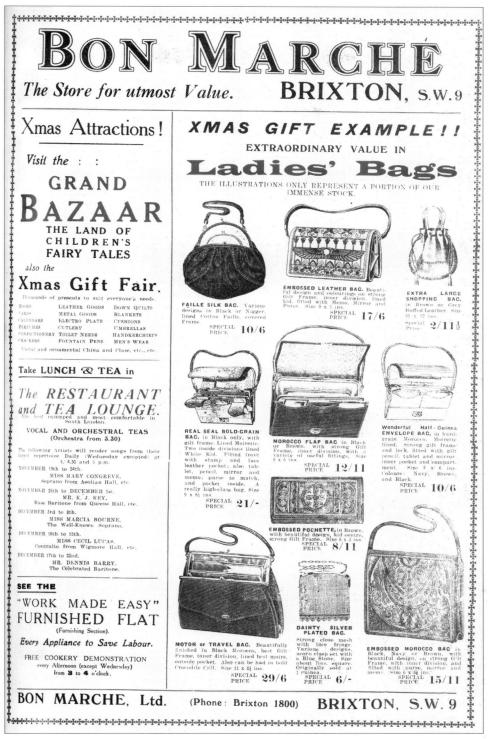

Bon Marché in 1924. In 1876 James Smith, a local businessman, won a large sum of money on the horses. He used it to construct Britain's first purpose-built department store, Bon Marché, on land previously occupied by market gardens in Brixton. The store became the centrepiece of a large and thriving shopping centre.

Pascal Street in the 1930s. Pascal Street stood between the Nine Elms goods depot and Wandsworth Road, one of the borough's poorest and most overcrowded streets. It was cleared in 1936 and replaced by the Hemans Estate.

Lockyer House, Hemans Street. This estate replaced the miserable slums of Hemans, Fount and Pascal Streets. This particular block, named after Lambeth's wartime mayor, was not completed until 1949 although it was still built to 1930s specifications.

Pullman Court, Streatham Hill. Built in 1935, it is typical of private apartment blocks of the time and boasted its own swimming pool. Tudor Close, further north on Brixton Hill, is another example.

An aerial view of Streatham Hill in the 1930s, showing the newly developed west side. Here can be seen the Streatham Hill Theatre, the Gaumont Palace cinema and the Locarno dance hall, these buildings earning Streatham the title of 'entertainment centre of South London'.

The Brixton Astoria cinema opened in 1929 with an ornate interior typical of the time. Picturegoers were transported into an Italianate garden with a balcony under a moonlit sky. The cinema became a music venue in the 1970s and is now the Brixton Academy.

The corner of Brixton and Stockwell Roads, *c.* 1932. Quin & Axtens, with Bon Marché and Morley's, was Brixton's third department store. The shop started small but gradually expanded to cover the whole of the parade between Ferndale and Stockwell Roads. Quin & Axtens was destroyed by bombing in 1941.

The front room of 11 Corrance Road in 1930, a typical suburban interior complete with gramophone, aspidistra and telephone.

Sailing toy boats and fishing for tiddlers on Clapham Common, *c.* 1933.

A diving competition at Brockwell Park Lido. The Lido was built in 1937 at the height of the fashion for outdoor pursuits.

A dance to commemorate the anniversary of the Armistice at the Streatham Locarno, which was built in 1931.

Brixton Road in the early 1930s before the building line was brought forward.

Brixton Road, seen from the town hall, in 1936. The LCC were finding it increasingly difficult to restrain commercial development on the long frontages to the houses on the east side of Brixton Road. The land was part of Rush Common and building was therefore prohibited. An agreement was reached in 1935, however, and the building line was brought forward. In this picture the old Prince of Wales and Barclays Bank can be seen, with the partially constructed new buildings in front. The project also enabled the building of a new art deco Woolworth's store, replacing the old shop on the corner of Atlantic Road.

Girls from Eardley Road School on Constitution Hill awaiting the arrival of the King and Queen, May 1935.

Mayor Hunter reads the proclamation of the abdication of Edward VIII on the steps of Lambeth Town Hall in 1936. Note that most people in the crowd are wearing a hat.

A street party to celebrate the Silver Jubilee of George V and Queen Mary, held in Coin Street in 1935. Souvenirs in the shape of spoons for girls and pocket knives for boys were distributed among Lambeth school children and 2,500 of the borough's aged poor were entertained at the Crystal Palace.

The Crystal Palace fire, 30 November 1936. A small fire in a staff lavatory went unchecked and spread so rapidly that the palace was destroyed beyond repair. The burning palace could be seen from the south coast. Nearly half the London Fire Brigade fought to put out the fire but they were seriously hampered by sightseers. The two water towers, built to supply the fountains, survived but were demolished in 1940 because they were obvious landmarks for enemy bombers.

The Rookery, Streatham Common, in the late 1930s. A scene of gentle suburban calm on a sunny day. Are the newspapers full of the impending war? The snoozing dog certainly doesn't seem to care.

Chapter 3
Lambeth at War

A war savings campaign. A motley crew of ARP Light Rescue volunteers are urging the people of Lambeth to buy war savings vouchers and 'make the blighter bend' during Warship Week in March 1942.

Lambeth, in common with the other inner London boroughs, suffered heavily during the war: 4,500 houses were destroyed and over 38,000 damaged, while 1,500 people were killed and nearly 3,000 seriously injured.

In 1939 air raid precautions were in full swing. Staff at the town hall and six of the public libraries worked round the clock assembling, fitting and issuing 220,000 gas masks. Almost every household was offered a choice of air raid shelters. Anderson shelters were a pit dug in the garden with a roof of corrugated iron covered with earth. By the end of 1939 12,000 Anderson shelters had been dug in Lambeth homes. Morrison shelters consisted of a steel cage inside the house that could withstand the collapse of a building. Public shelters were constructed in streets, trench shelters were dug in most of the parks and open spaces in the borough. The basements of public buildings, shops and factories were also turned into shelters.

Evacuation of children and expectant mothers from London began in earnest in early September, just as war was declared. Even though less than 50 per cent of London children registered for evacuation, over 1.5 million set off on Green Line buses and underground trains to suburban railway stations. The main railway termini were not used; special trains took the evacuees to reception areas all over the south-east. Schools were largely kept together: for instance Sudbourne School was sent to Brighton, St Luke's, Norwood, to Goring-by-Sea. Trains were simply filled up and despatched, so many families and friends were separated.

Then nothing much happened. The period known as the 'Phoney War', when the Germans were concentrating on France and the Low Countries, plunged Britain into a bewildering calm. The ARP service had plenty of time for intensive training and exercises. Over half of the children evacuated at the beginning of the war returned to London and schools and nurseries began to reopen.

The attacks began at the end of August 1940. Eleven incidents were reported on the night of 29 August in the Loughborough Road and Gipsy Hill areas. Foreign Street off Lilford Road can lay claim to the dubious honour of receiving the first bomb. As the Battle of Britain raged over London, high explosive and incendiary bombs devastated Lambeth. Thousands of people were made homeless. Lambeth Council opened rest centres in schools and church halls around the borough and houses were requisitioned and turned into flats to rehouse displaced families.

Two of the most serious incidents in Lambeth happened on the same night, 15 October, when Morley College and the Kennington Park trench shelter received direct hits. Morley College, on Westminster Bridge Road, had been taken over a fortnight before as a rest and feeding centre for those rendered homeless after the bombing of flats on Hercules Road and Carlisle Lane. Assisted by volunteers from the nearby Lady Margaret Hall Settlement, the gymnasium had been turned into a dormitory and shelter. Some more families, victims of another incident, had been moved in, bringing the numbers up to 250. On the night of 15 October about a third of these people had gone to the Tube for shelter, leaving around 200 in the building. At 7.45 p.m. a bomb fell through the roof of the college and exploded above the restaurant, where people were preparing to sleep. Many people were trapped between floors as the building collapsed into the basement. Rescue parties worked through the night while bombs continued to fall. The Morley College caretaker was able to accelerate the rescue operation by identifying those parts of the building used as dormitories. Of the 195 people in the building, 57 of them died, and the last two casualties were not recovered from the rubble until twenty days later.

The Kennington Park trench shelter was hit on the same night, a substantial portion of it collapsing completely. Rescue parties struggled to free survivors while more bombs fell on the park. In all fifty-six people were killed.

As I read the incident reports in the borough's archive fifty years later I was shocked and moved. Those like myself, with parents who lived through the war, often know little of the realities of the bombing. The horrors were not spoken of when I was a child in the 1960s. I formed my images of the bombing from funny stories about neighbours being blown out of their baths into the street and from films and TV programmes about everyone pulling together. Only when I read the incident reports and the accounts of the air raid wardens did I get a real sense of what war was really like for civilians. Stanley Rothwell, in his excellent *Lambeth at War*, writes of his experiences as an air raid warden in Lambeth. He sums up the reality of war for the people of Lambeth in this moving final passage:

We had been detailed to West Norwood, there was a heavy casualty list there which we cleared. On our way back we could hear the oncoming doodle bug behind us chugging like a motor bike, in front of us on a rise we saw two semi-detached houses. A man was digging his garden alongside, a little boy was running up the garden path towards the house, his schoolbag slung across his shoulder. At the door a woman was beckoning to him to hurry indoors. The engine of the flying bomb shut off, We crouched waiting for the crunch. It glided over and past us and settled on the two houses all in a space of seconds. There was a loud explosion, a mushroom cloud of dust. Everything went up; no houses, no man, no mother and no boy. We picked up three dustbins full of pieces from the rubble. The only way to identify where they were was the dampening dust and the clouds of flies.

The evacuation of patients from St Thomas's Hospital, September 1939.

Children from St Luke's School, West Norwood, evacuated to Goring-by-Sea, Sussex, in 1939. After widespread preparation and evacuation the bombers failed to arrive until late 1940. By this time the majority of evacuated children had returned home.

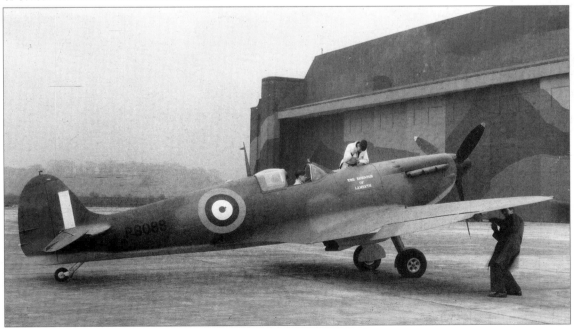

The Borough of Lambeth Spitfire. As a morale-boosting and fund-raising measure, the people of Lambeth were invited to subscribe towards the cost of a Spitfire. Subscribers were kept in touch with the progress of the aeroplane through a newsletter.

King George VI and Queen Elizabeth visit the Duchy of Cornwall Estate in Kennington, March 1940.

The opening of the Information and Administrative Centre in Acre Lane, January 1942. The man on the left is Henry Willinck MP, Commissioner for the Rehousing of Homeless Persons in London, and next to him is Bill Lockyer, who was Mayor of Lambeth throughout the war. The centre was totally destroyed by a V1 flying bomb in June 1944, when twenty-one people were killed.

Civil Defence Sunday, November 1942. Civil Defence wardens pass Mayor Lockyer and Mr Roberts, the town clerk, at the saluting base outside Lambeth Town Hall.

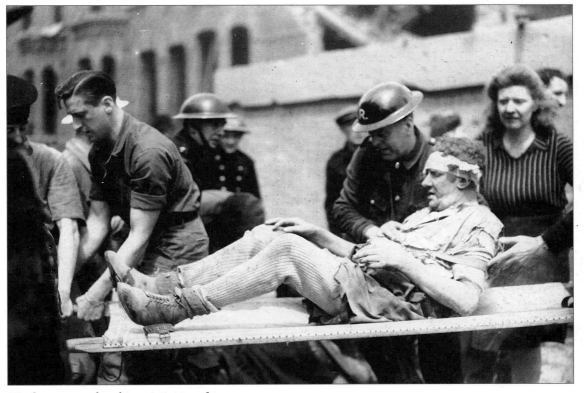

Wardens carry a bombing victim to safety.

Beechdale Road, Brixton Hill, after a flying bomb fell on Nos 67 to 76 in June 1944. Six people were killed, many more injured, and the impact of the blast was felt as far as Upper Tulse Hill.

The Lord Mayor of London, Sir Frank Newson Smith, visits bombed-out residents of Beechdale Road, 1944.

A model of HMS *Diomedes*, Lambeth's adopted battleship, during War Weapons Week, 1942.

Bombed flats at Kennington Oval, 24 August 1944.

A Mobile Information Unit, *c.* 1941. Lambeth was the first borough in the London region to have a MBIU; these units announced emergency arrangements by loudspeaker immediately after an air raid.

Salvage operations begin in Effra Parade, July 1944.

Living under tarpaulins. This was the reality of wartime bombing, with thousands of people made homeless and having to get their lives back to normal as best they could.

Holy Trinity School, Lutheran Place, was devastated by bombing in 1940. The school was rebuilt after the war on a new site on Upper Tulse Hill.

St Thomas's Hospital, Westminster Bridge. The hospital was bombed at least six times during the Second World War, including two flying bomb hits in 1944. No patients were killed but ten staff lost their lives. The hospital never closed entirely and an emergency operating theatre was set up in the basement. The Westminster Bridge blocks that were very badly damaged were demolished. In the middle of the devastation the statue of Edward VI survived intact, and now stands at the entrance to the modern building.

Lilian Rolfe, alias Nadine or Claudie, who fought with the Special Operations Executive in France. Her family lived in Knatchbull and Paulet Roads. She was dropped by parachute into occupied France and worked to secure radio links until she was captured by the Gestapo. She was executed at Ravensbruck concentration camp alongside Violette Szabo in 1945.

The chic raincoats and berets belong to the women of the French Forces of the Interior, who visited Lambeth in November 1944. They are seen here politely pretending to enjoy a cup of tea at the mobile canteen.

Temporary housing at Loughborough Gardens, January 1945. These makeshift homes were built by American engineers.

The Oval cricket ground, 1945. The Oval was requisitioned in 1939 and initially used as a site for anti-aircraft guns and searchlights. It was then prepared as a prisoner-of-war camp but never used. Although the ground was not hit directly many bombs fell in the immediate area. The men seen here are removing posts set in 2 ft of concrete from the outfield. By the end of the war the ground was completely overgrown and a mass of gaping holes and trenches. Miraculously the groundsman, Bert Lock, and his team repaired the damage and the 1946 season opened as if nothing had happened.

The Lambeth baths incident. On 4 January 1945 the baths received a direct hit from a V2 rocket and were damaged beyond repair. The top view is from Morton Place looking across Lambeth Road and shows the full extent of the damage to the baths and surrounding housing. Thirty-seven people died as a result of the bombing; most of them were from Surrey Lodge in Lambeth Road.

Brockwell Park Open Air Theatre, *c.* 1942. The small child in the foreground, watching a performance of *The Gondoliers* by the D'Oyly Carte Company, is the author's mother.

A wheelbarrow fire pump. This picture was taken at the Lambeth Civil Defence Centre in Norwood.

War Weapons Week, 1942. Mayor and Mrs Lockyer are standing with Councillor Simpson on the steps of Lambeth Town Hall. Bill Lockyer was Mayor of Lambeth throughout the war years.

A bombed-out train in north Lambeth. These trains were used to take corpses to Brookwood Cemetery.

People stare into a bomb crater in Kennington Lane, July 1944.

Rescue services at Waterloo, with County Hall in the background, June 1944.

A victory parade in Brixton, seen from Lambeth Town Hall, in 1945. The parade ran from Crystal Palace to Brixton.

Cadets and wardens queue for the victory service in St Matthew's church, Brixton, 1945.

The children of Lower Marsh Infants School receive toys from Australia, 1945.

Comedians Jewell and Warriss visit Lambeth Town Hall to promote welfare food supplements, *c.* 1947.

Chapter 4
Brave New World

Lambeth councillors doing the Lambeth Walk during a visit to Vincennes, France, 1950s. Town twinning was all the rage in the postwar period and Lambeth was twinned with Vincennes and Moskvaretsky, a suburb of Moscow.

In 1947 Elsie Boltz of the North Lambeth Labour Party, later Lambeth's first woman mayoress, complained bitterly to the BBC. *Down Your Way*, the popular radio programme, had claimed to feature Lambeth but had ventured no further than Lambeth Walk. 'The borough isn't entirely composed of loud mouthed cockneys', said the outraged Mrs Boltz. A flood of letters to the South London Press sang the praises of the more 'refined' parts of the borough. As others questioned the outdated image of cheerful costers dancing their troubles away in pie and mash shops. It was time for a change: Lambeth had been devastated by the war and needed to be taken seriously.

The postwar period was one of drastic change, both in the physical appearance of the borough and in its population. The effect of the bombing on London's housing was catastrophic and Lambeth was no exception. New housing was an overriding priority for the council and the LCC. The homeless situation was acute and there was a shortage of both building materials and a workforce. Architectural visions were abandoned and pre-war designs were adapted using any available material. Over 1,000 prefabricated houses were installed around the borough. The first estate to be completed by Lambeth Council was the extension of the Hemans Street Estate off Wandsworth Road, where the foundations had been laid before the war. The Studley Estate in Stockwell came next, followed by the Holderness Estate in Norwood. The LCC built the St Martin's Estate in 1954 and Loughborough Estate in 1957.

Lambeth had always had people of many different nationalities among its population but the years following the war saw changes that set the foundations of the multicultural Lambeth of today. There were substantial communities of Poles, Cypriots and Italians; Brixton, especially, had a substantial and highly visible Jewish population, with many Jewish local politicians and business people. There was a strong anti-fascist element in Brixton: in 1947 Lambeth Council banned meetings in Rushcroft Road after clashes with the Mosleyite 'British League of Ex-Servicemen' and anti-fascists. There were black people living in Lambeth long before the war but they were few and far between, remembered as personalities and individuals.

In the aftermath of the Second World War troop ships sailed around the world depositing and picking up servicemen and civilians. The first of these to pass through the Caribbean was the SS *Empire Windrush* in 1948. The *Windrush* picked up about 500 West Indians and brought them to England. Those who had nowhere to live were accommodated in the deep shelters on Clapham Common. Some houses in Somerleyton, Geneva and Mostyn Roads had been owned by West Indians and West Africans since the 1930s and some of the settlers naturally went there in search of accommodation and a sympathetic face.

The fall in population after the war had resulted in a labour shortage and people from the West Indies were encouraged in newspaper advertisements by London Transport and British Rail to come to Britain to work. Contrary to popular myth they were not expecting the streets to be paved with gold: wartime experience had showed many of them the reality of life in Britain. Marcus Lipton, Brixton's MP, welcomed them in a reception at the Astoria and urged them to 'regard this country as your second home. I hope that it will not be very long before each of you is provided for in a dignified fashion.'

There were no race riots in Brixton as there were in Notting Hill and Nottingham but any incident in Brixton was played up by the national press. That doesn't mean there wasn't any racism. Scanning through the small ads in the South London Press of the 1950s gives an idea of how difficult it was for black people to find rented accommodation. Phrases such as 'No coloured', 'European references only', 'whites only' appear with depressing regularity. The Streatham Locarno insisted that for their Monday night rock and roll dance 'coloured men are requested to bring a lady partner and are welcomed only on this condition'. The 1960s saw an influx of African people, particularly students from the new independent states, and later political refugees.

After the harsh years of the war the people of Lambeth needed to enjoy themselves again and the local authorities took a leading role in this. The postwar years are marked by festivals and parades, exhibitions and outings. Lambeth's south bank had become an embarrassing eyesore. Decline in industry along the river front had left many buildings derelict and heavy bombing had finished off the rest. It was an ideal site for the Festival of Britain, Herbert Morrison's celebration of Britain's achievements, in 1951. Staged to commemorate the centenary of the Great Exhibition, the festival was welcomed as a reawakening after years of austerity. The derelict India Stores, the Lion Brewery and the bombed warehouses were replaced by the Festival Hall, the Dome of Discovery and the Skylon. Eight million people visited the festival, wandered through the futuristic (in a Dan Dare sort of way) landscape, marvelled at pavilions entitled 'Land and People' and 'Power and Production' and shrieked their way through the rides at the Festival Gardens along the river at Battersea.

The festival was a potent symbol of the new age. Roy Strong, celebrating the twenty-fifth anniversary of the festival, wrote: 'the festival style belongs firmly and squarely to the world of the New Towns, to the piazzas and pedestrian precincts, the espresso bars and community centres, to the blocks of council flats and the rows of little houses and, above all, to the office buildings of the idea it expressed most, that of the postwar welfare state'. That description also sums up the vision of the postwar borough councils, including Lambeth.

A greengrocer's cart outside prefabs in Brixton, *c.* 1948. By 1951 over a thousand prefabricated houses had been erected in the borough, an attempt to alleviate the critical housing situation. They were only supposed to be used for a short time but many survived for another thirty years.

A pageant as part of the Lambeth Festival celebrations on the steps of Lambeth Town Hall in 1951. After the horrors of the war and the subsequent austerity, there was a whole series of festivals, pageants and exhibitions staged by the council in an attempt to lift the spirits of the people of Lambeth.

A civil defence food preparation exercise in the 1950s.

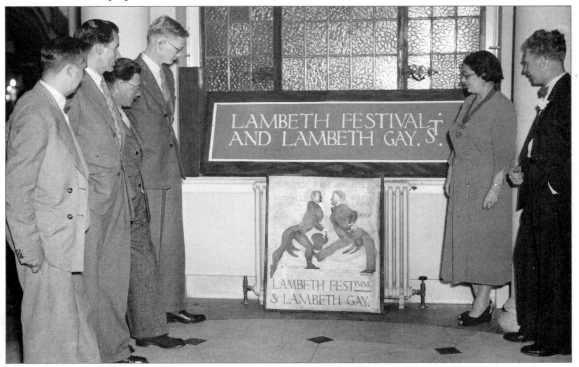

Lambeth Festival and Lambeth Gay, 1951. Lambeth's first woman mayor, Elsie Boltz, entertaining a group of nice young men in the town hall.

Boys playing on a bomb site in Waterloo, 1947. This photograph gives a good impression of the surreal landscape created by the war.

The Albert Embankment from Lambeth Bridge, 1948. The riverside industry had declined and been superseded by offices. On the exteme left is the new Doulton's building, beside it the white brick headquarters of W.H. Smith, the headquarters of the London Fire Brigade and the old Doulton's headquarters, bombed and semi-derelict.

A bewildered group of tourists gather in the shadow of the Coade stone lion outside Waterloo station, in 1950. This photograph was taken from an album recording the building of the Shell Centre. The lion originally stood on top of the Lion Brewery building on the South Bank. When the brewery was demolished to make way for the Festival of Britain site, the lion was placed outside the station. In 1966 it was moved to its present home at the foot of Westminster Bridge.

The filming of *Passport to Pimlico*, 1948. The derelict north of the borough was also an ideal film set.

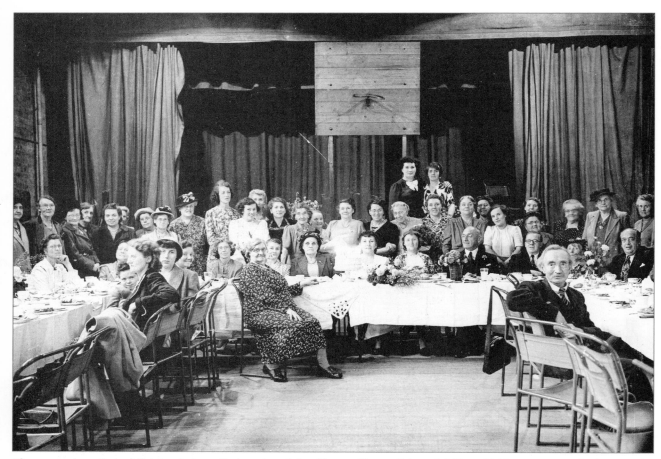

The women's section of Brixton Labour Party entertaining Marcus Lipton, Brixton's MP, in 1947. He was Lambeth Council's first Jewish alderman and a fervent anti-fascist. He represented Brixton from 1945, when he was still in the army, until his death in 1978. In the centre of the picture is Mary Marock, who was a well-known figure in postwar Brixton. She was secretary of Brixton Labour Party, a Lambeth councillor, Mayoress of Lambeth in 1955 and founder member of the Brixton Darby and Joan Club.

Alfie Howard, Lambeth's town crier. Still in post at the age of eighty-six as this book is written, Alfie was appointed in 1946. He has visited over sixty-one countries, met four US presidents and appeared on the *Johnny Carson Show* eight times. He has also appeared on stage with Jayne Mansfield and sung a duet with Tom Jones, still finding plenty of time for official functions and commendable charity work.

Mayor Simpson shows his regalia to a group of German schoolgirls who visited Lambeth in 1949.

Aneurin Bevan with Mayor Simpson on the town hall steps during the 'Our Lambeth' exhibition in 1949.

The Brixton Falcon Roller Skating Club on their float at the Lambeth Festival of 1951. The roller skating rink, on the corner of Tulse Hill and Water Lane, opened in 1910 and was a popular meeting place for fifty-five years. The rink finally closed in 1965 and the site is now occupied by a carpet warehouse.

The South Bank during the Festival of Britain, 1951. This stretch of the river bank had become very unattractive, full of derelict and bombed warehouses. It was the ideal site for Herbert Morrison's Festival. The shot tower, dating from 1826, was turned into a lighthouse. Next to the newly built Royal Festival Hall is the Dome of Discovery, which looks like a scaled-down Millennium Dome. Not such a coincidence: Herbert Morrison was the grandfather of Peter Mandelson.

Gracie Fields entertains Lambeth pensioners at the Festival Hall during Lambeth Festival Week, 1951.

Fireworks on the South Bank celebrating the coronation of Queen Elizabeth II in 1953.

Streatham Hill railway station bedecked with coronation bunting in 1953.

Lambeth Walk in 1953.

A dancing display in Brockwell Park.

Brixton celebrates the coronation as crowds gather to watch the parades in 1953.

New arrivals from the West Indies waiting at customs at Southampton in the 1950s. Labour shortages after the war prompted organizations such as London Transport to encourage West Indians to come to Britain to work.

Somerleyton Road, Brixton. Some of the houses in this road were already owned by black people and the new arrivals, finding many white landlords hostile, sought accommodation among their own kind.

Local boy made good, Charlie Chaplin, visits Lambeth Town Hall in 1953. He had just presented Mayor Wallace with a cheque for £2,000 for the poor of Lambeth.

The inevitable crowd gathers around an argument between a market inspector and an illegal street trader in Electric Lane, Brixton, 1952. As Brixton market expanded into Electric Avenue, and shopkeepers objected to the noise and rubbish, the council clamped down on itinerant street traders.

Electric Avenue in August 1960.

W.H. Smith's newspaper stand at Streatham Hill station, 1955.

Dainty teas and luncheons at the York Cottage tea rooms, Streatham High Road, 1958.

A still very Victorian-looking Brixton reference library in the 1950s.

A postwar Lambeth street scene. This photograph was used by the council as a typical example of slum housing.

A site reserved for the building of a council estate in the 1950s. Slum clearance and bombing ensured that Lambeth's landscape, especially in the north of the borough, changed beyond recognition.

No. 44 Poynders Road, shortly before its demolition in 1950. Many of the surviving houses of Thomas Cubitt's Clapham Park development of the 1840s were demolished during this period to make way for the Clapham Park housing estate.

Slum housing in Lyric Place, Kennington, demolished to build the Opal Street development in the 1950s.

Mayor Simpson makes a speech at the opening of the Portobello Estate, West Norwood, 1949. The estate was built on the site of Portobello House on Knights Hill. The cedar trees and an ornamental lake were preserved. The estate was a mixed development of flats and houses, with a fully mechanized laundry and special units for elderly and single people. Presumably the loudspeaker van had been hired to rally the crowds.

The Holderness Estate on Knights Hill, in the process of being built in 1952.

Flats in Opal Street, Kennington, 1952.

A typical council flat interior of the early 1950s.

The Denmark Road Estate. This was another development that was begun in the 1930s and delayed by the war. The blocks were given names with Danish connections: Elsinore, Mercia, Norse, Dane, Viking and Zealand.

An old man surveys the Corbusian slabs of the LCC's Loughborough Estate. An extension to the estate won a Civic Trust award in 1961.

The Hop Poles public house, Upper Tulse Hill, shortly before redevelopment in the late 1960s.

Burrough's pie and mash shop in Lambeth Walk. Pie, mash and eels are no longer standard working-class fare and few of these shops now survive. Burrough's also had a shop in Coldharbour Lane, Brixton, which is now a Japanese noodle bar.

The Dick Sheppard school orchestra, cellos at the ready, *c.* 1956. The Dick Sheppard school opened in September 1955 with places for a thousand girls. The school had four different houses represented by different coloured jumpers – red, blue, green and yellow.

The Baker sisters with their snowman in the garden of 78 Endymion Road in the winter of 1962.

Brixton Road in the 1960s with two blasts from the past, a 2A bus and a rag-and-bone man.

A beauty contest, possibly at the Assembly Hall, Acre Lane. Curiously, each number is shared by a black and a white contestant.

The Locarno, Streatham, was a major dance venue in South London. A few doors away the Gaumont cinema had become a bowling alley and the Streatham Hill Theatre had turned into a bingo hall.

Streatham Astoria, later the Odeon, in the 1960s. Built in the 1930s in the form of an Egyptian temple with an elaborately decorated restaurant, the Astoria was one of a new wave of super-cinemas.

Brixton market in the 1960s.

An oddity from the council's public relations department. A woman, dressed only in a shirt, standing in Tate Library Gardens, surrounded by travel brochures. Why?

A Clapham High Street clothes shop, *c.* 1962, in the days when it was safe to leave babies outside shops.

Lambeth Walk, 1965. Bombing had ripped the heart out of the famous market and it was never the same again. In the late 1960s the GLC embarked on a wholesale redevelopment of the area.

Chapter 5
Loony Lambeth and Beyond

A jubilant Ted Knight with Lambeth councillors on the steps of Lambeth Town Hall, having refused to set a rate, 7 March 1985. Rate capping had been introduced by the Thatcher government as a means to control highspending local authorities. The eighteen councils concerned, with Lambeth at the forefront, argued against the resultant loss of jobs and services. William Waldegrave, undersecretary of state for the environment, branded them 'childish polytechnic Marxists spending money on gays'.

One by one the other councils set a rate until Lambeth stood alone. Finally, in July, a councillor's resignation broke the majority and a rate was set. The days of 'Red Ted' were numbered.

T he 1970s and 1980s were periods of protest and conflict, a transition from the radical '60s to the sensible '90s. This was also when Lambeth gained its 'loony left' tag and became the scourge of the national press. The story of this period is a book in itself, or possibly several.

Lambeth Council had been Labour-controlled since 1934, so it was a shock to the system when a Conservative majority was elected in 1968. In many ways they were more radical than the previous Labour administration. The Director of Housing, Harry Simpson, had forced a change of heart in the housing policy by taking Tory councillors, including a young John Major, on a visit to the poorest black families in central Brixton. This had such an impression that they quadrupled the housing programme inherited from Labour. Nevertheless Labour were re-elected in 1971.

Meanwhile things were changing in the local Labour Party. The old guard were dying off and being replaced by a new wave of younger and more radical activists such as Ken Livingstone and Ted Knight. By 1978 the left were in control of the council.

This did not happen in isolation. Lambeth, like other inner-city areas such as Hackney and Islington, had become a focus for change. Black activists, civil rights campaigners, feminist groups, gay activists and squatters groups all naturally gravitated to places like Lambeth where they were welcomed, not just by a sympathetic local authority but by a largely unfazed population.

Tension was growing in Brixton. Unemployment, especially among black youths, was high and the police had recently introduced a vigorous 'stop and search' campaign to combat rising crime figures. On Friday 10 April 1981 a policeman attempted to stop a young man in Atlantic Road who had been stabbed in the back. The man resisted and fled to a nearby flat, where the occupants dressed his wounds and called him a cab. A police van stopped the cab, examined the man and called an ambulance. A crowd of black youths had by now gathered around the man and assumed he was being arrested. They seized him, flagged down a passing car and told the driver to take the man to hospital. The crowd had now grown to about a hundred, who were pursued by the police. Minor scuffles broke out but it was all over by early evening.

On the Saturday afternoon two plainclothes policemen attempted to search a minicab driver for drugs in Railton Road. An angry crowd gathered, and a struggle ensued in which a man was arrested. As the police van took the man away bricks were thrown, the crowd grew bigger and there followed the worst violence Brixton has ever seen. Cars were burnt, shops were set on fire or looted, a local school was burnt down and emergency services were denied access by the crowds. The trouble continued into the Sunday and Monday, when there were minor skirmishes.

Rene Webb, former chair of the Lambeth Community Relations Council, told the *Sunday Times*: 'This has set the cause of race relations in South London back twenty years. These kids are furious with the police and they will carry on until the cops go home. I have lived in Brixton since the war and this is the greatest tragedy ever to befall this area.' Figures from a monitoring exercise by Lambeth Law Centre made a mockery of claims that these were race riots with black against white and that agitators from outside Brixton had organized the riots. Only 65 per cent of those arrested during the disturbances were black and 90 per cent came from the Brixton area.

The Home Secretary Willie Whitelaw ordered an immediate inquiry into the causes of the rioting, to be headed by Lord Scarman. Ted Knight called for an amnesty for those arrested during the disturbances. Courtney Laws of the Brixton Neighbourhood Community Association dismissed claims that the riots were started by outsiders and urged young blacks to reject the overtures of political extremists who were trying to exploit the situation.

A year later the West Indian World commemorated the anniversary of the riots with 'hope and disappointment'. They described local and central government initiatives as 'like spitting on a red hot poker to cool it down'. Even so, they sensed a clear determination by Brixton's black community to put the events of April 1981 behind them and move on.

The Rates Act of 1984 enabled the Secretary of State to identify 'high spending' councils and limit their rate for the next financial year. Councils like Lambeth, who had chosen not to cut services or jobs but to increase the rates, were put to the test. Eighteen authorities, all but two of them Labour-controlled, were identified for ratecapping. A strategy of non-compliance was put forward, consisting of councils deferring the setting of a rate for the next financial year, and was endorsed by the Labour Party Conference.

Then it all went pear-shaped. On 7 March, the day after anti-ratecapping demonstrations had taken place around the country, the Inner London Educational Authority set a rate. The GLC followed three days later. Over the next three months all except Lambeth set a rate. Then, on 10 July, two Lambeth Labour councillors pushed through a legal rate with the backing of the Tories. Thirty-one Lambeth councillors were disqualified and surcharged.

In 1989 Lambeth hit the headlines again with the controversy over the Vauxhall by-election. Stuart Holland, the Labour MP for Vauxhall, unexpectedly resigned in order to take up a European research post. There was strong pressure for the party to select a black candidate but the Labour Party National Executive found the shortlist unacceptable and imposed their own choice, Kate Hoey. Outrage ensued, inspiring the wonderful newspaper headline, 'Hoey hooey won't go away'. The by-election developed into a media circus. There were fourteen contenders for the seat, including two independent black candidates, but Kate Hoey won with an increased majority. Controversy continued in the early 1990s when a group of Lambeth councillors were expelled from the Labour Party.

The focus then turned to the council itself. An independent inquiry by Elizabeth Appleby QC brought to light serious irregularities in highways maintenance and housing repair contracts. In April 1995 Heather Rabbatts became Lambeth's Chief Executive with a 'mission impossible', to turn Lambeth into a reliable and responsible local authority. She didn't mince words: 'Failure to collect income and manage its finances, a shambles in housing repairs and litter strewn streets, failure to control contracts – this is Lambeth's history.'

A doggedly New Labour council was elected in 1998. Now, at the time of writing, the emphasis is on providing quality public service while balancing the books. This is a time of enormous change; the council and its departments are virtually unrecognizable from ten years ago. Regeneration of blighted parts of the borough such as Brixton, Streatham and Vauxhall is high on the agenda. An era of hope and determination has emerged with local people and councillors pinning their hopes on the dynamic reputation of the Chief Executive. Only time will tell.

The Streatham Locarno became The Cat's Whiskers in 1970, in an attempt to move with the times, and offered chicken in a basket and a nightly cabaret.

The Lambeth Country Show, Brockwell Park, in the mid-1970s, judging by the width of the trousers and the Chopper bikes.

Lambeth librarians storytelling on the Cowley Estate, *c*. 1972. These were the days when librarians went out to parks and council estates to encourage children to read.

An adventure playground on a north Lambeth estate in 1978.

Motorbike stunts, Evel Knievel style, at Lambeth Country Show in 1976.

The Silver Blades ice rink, Streatham. This was where I did my socializing, aged thirteen, on Saturday afternoons, to the sounds of *Alice Cooper, Sweet* and *Gary Glitter*. The fashion was for high-waisted, side-pocketed Trevira flares that draped over the skates and skimmed the ice. By the end of the afternoon the water had seeped halfway up our trouser legs.

110

Councillor John Major addresses the council chamber, Lambeth Town Hall, 1971. Many Lambeth councillors have gone on to become MPs, including Ken Livingstone, Tony Banks and Peter Mandelson, but only one has been Prime Minister.

A domino club at the Assembly Hall, Acre Lane, Brixton, in the 1970s.

An anti-Nazi demonstration, Brixton, *c.* 1978. With the rise of the National Front and the British Movement in the 1970s, areas with large immigrant populations like Brixton were targeted. In response there was a massive and popular anti-fascist campaign with the Anti-Nazi League and Rock Against Racism holding demonstrations and open-air concerts, including a number in Brockwell Park. There was a whole series of badges to collect: 'Women against the Nazis', 'Schoolkids against the Nazis', even 'Skateboarders against the Nazis'.

A fire-eater captivates onlookers at the Waterloo Festival in 1976.

Members of a local women's group making a video, The Cut, 1976.

A north Lambeth garage in the 1980s.

A boxing match at the Waterloo Festival of 1978.

The Harlem Globetrotters visit Lambeth. They can be seen here at the Flaxman sports centre in 1979.

A good time is certainly had by all at the 1979 Waterloo Festival.

The Brixton riots of April 1981. The weekend
of 10 April saw the worst violence ever in
Brixton, with cars and buses wrecked,
buildings set on fire and widescale looting of
shops. The Scarman Report, commissioned by
the government to investigate the cause of the
riots, blamed deprivation and discrimination
but concluded, 'The police do not create social
deprivation or racial disadvantage: they are
not responsible for the disadvantages of the
ethnic minorities. Yet their role is crucial. . . .
If they neglect consultation and co-operation
with the local community unrest is certain
and riot becomes probable.'

The remains of Scotties Boutique in Coldharbour Lane on the morning after the riots.

Clearing up the debris in Electric Avenue.

Anna Tapsell, Lambeth NALGO Chair, speaks at an anti-cuts rally in 1984 watched by Ken Livingstone and Ted Knight, before they fell out over ratecapping in the 1980s.

Lambeth NALGO demonstrating in central London in the 1980s.

Lambeth councillors singing the 'Red Flag', 7 May 1985. In the front row, from left to right, are Councillors Boateng, Smith, Warburton, Knight, McPherson-Quinn and Phipp.

Lambeth at the High Court, supported by Liverpool councillors Hatton and Mulhearn on the right of the picture.

Brixton in the 1980s. The riots were a turning point for Brixton. The spotlight turned on to the deprivation in inner-city areas that was seen to be the cause of the trouble. The 'I'm Backing Brixton' campaign was an attempt to bring back businesses that had left the area after the rioting. In the 1990s the Brixton Challenge Company was set up to administer the spending of City Challenge money given by the government to regenerate the area. The company ended its five-year stint in 1998 amid allegations of poor management but, whoever was responsible, Brixton has seen many improvements over the last ten years. It now boasts a theatre, an arthouse cinema, a major music venue as well as an alarming number of busy restaurants and bars. It also has a thriving arts community with at least three art galleries and a Sunday arts market.

119

Lambeth Walk, 1990. Redeveloped by the GLC in the 1970s the market survives in rather bleak surroundings.

Brockwell Park Lido in 1961 and 1996. Built by the LCC in 1937, it is a monument to 1930s municipal idealism. The pool has had a renaissance in the 1990s and boasts a restaurant and regular poolside barbecues. A recent television film showed the Lido as an alternative wedding venue.

West Norwood cemetery. Formerly the South Metropolitan cemetery, West Norwood was opened in 1839, one of the great Victorian showpiece graveyards. It has many illustrious residents including the Sir Henries Tate, Doulton and Bessemer and Mrs Beeton. Despite a controversial programme of grave destruction by Lambeth Council in the 1970s it remains a glorious monument to the Victorian obsession with mortality.

Brixton Synagogue in the early 1990s. Brixton's Jewish community played a prominent role in business and local politics, especially in the postwar years. The closing of the synagogue in 1981 reflected the dwindling Jewish population, who had largely moved south to Streatham. The synagogue was opened in 1921 and the first rabbi was the father of Lord Mischon.

An apartment block on the corner of Clapham Common North Side and Cedars Road. Built in the 1880s by J.T. Knowles this is a perfect example of a building changing its use to reflect the fortunes of the area. Originally grandiose terraced homes it was used as a homeless reception centre in the 1970s and has now reverted to luxury apartments.

Brixton market. A nail-bomb attack by a racist extremist in April 1999 shocked the market to the core. However, the 'business as usual' ethos prevailed with stallholders and shoppers alike.

St Matthew's Peace Garden, 1990s. St Matthew's church was built in the 1820s when Brixton was still surrounded by countryside. The building is now used as a theatre, with a successful restaurant in the crypt.

Another remnant of old Brixton and certainly the most picturesque. Brixton windmill was built by the Ashby family in 1816 and remained in use by the same family until 1934.

Linda Bellos, leader of Lambeth Council in the late 1980s, seen here helping out the binmen.

Anti-poll tax demonstrators in Acre Lane in 1990.

Heather Rabbatts, Lambeth's troubleshooting Chief Executive, seen here with Elizabeth Appleby QC who led an inquiry into corruption and mismanagement in Lambeth.

Friday 12 July 1996, a proud day for Brixton when Nelson Mandela visited the recreation centre. He came there with Prince Charles, who must have felt a little sidelined.

Acknowledgements

Thank you to the following for the use of their photographs (page no, u = upper, l = lower):

p. 14u, London Metropolitan Archives; p. 17l, Penny Hatfield; pp. 18u, 37l, Devall family; p. 25u, St George's Hospital; p. 27u, Rayson family; pp. 29u, 31u, 74l, 83u, 88l, Railtrack; pp. 30l, 42l, author; p. 39l, Patricia Jenkyns; p. 40ul, Lambeth Mission; pp. 41ul, 61u, St Luke's School; p. 42u, Surrey CCC Library; p. 51u, Mrs Emons; p. 69u, Tania Rolfe; p. 72u, Margaret Mckenzie; pp. 73l, 82u, Mr Gedge; p. 83l, Mr King; p. 110, Tamar Baker; pp. 90u, 101l, 110u, Mckenzie Heritage Picture Library; p. 103u © Val Wilmer; p. 103l, Mrs Stutchbury; pp. 105, 117ul, 118ul, Dave Stewart; pp. 114l, 115l, 116ul, Ray Wilkie; p. 124u, Maureen Manning; p. 125l, Rhoda Webb.

The remainder are from Lambeth Archives Department or are unsourced. Please note that every effort has been made to establish and contact copyright holders but this has not been possible in every case. If I have omitted to mention any individuals or organizations I offer my sincere apologies and thanks.

Sources
Text for this book has been researched almost entirely at Lambeth Archives Department. Extensive use has been made of the South London Press, council minutes and reports, official guides and cuttings. Secondary sources include:

Beryl Barrow, *Lambeth 1950–1970*, 1998.
Walter Besant, *London South of the Thames*, 1912.
Jill Dudman, *Lambeth, Kennington and Clapham in Old Photographs*, 1995.
Graham Gower, *History of Suburban Streatham*, 1996.
Ken Livingstone, *If they thought voting would change anything, they'd abolish it*, 1987.
London Borough of Lambeth / Black Cultural Archives, *The Windrush Legacy*, 1998.
Alan Piper, *History of Brixton*, 1996.
Survey of London, 1951.

INDEX